East vs West

How Differences in Thought Impact Our Understanding of Scripture

Dr. Bur Shilling

For additional biblical understanding or information go to

Kaleidoscope Ministries, LLC
www.burshilling.com

Printed in the United States of America

ISBN: 9798395032980

ACKNOWLEDGMENT

A special thank you to Dr. Charles R. Page II who thirty-five years ago launched my thinking into the differences between Eastern and Western thought and their impact on one's understanding of scripture. I look forward to adding to this list as I continue this journey.

Contents

Why Examine the Differences between Eastern Thinking and Western Thinking

Why is it often so difficult to understand the meaning of a biblical story or a teaching of Jesus? Perhaps it's because we don't understand that the Bible reflects Eastern thought and there are significant differences in attitudes and values between Eastern thinking and Western thinking.

In 1889, the English author Rudyard Kipling wrote the epic poem "The Ballad of East and West,"[1] which begins with the line, "Oh, East is East, and West is West, and Never the Twain Shall Meet."

This well describes the differences between the ancient Eastern mind and our current Western thought when it comes to understanding Scripture. Concepts such as logic and causality are perceived very differently in these two ways of thinking.

According to one author, these differences are the result of their respective cultures, based on their ancient systems of philosophy and education: China in the East; Greece in the West. "(The Eastern mind) views the world through a wide-angle lens, whereas Westerners have tunnel vision."[2]

This radical difference in perspective means that students of the Bible who want to truly understand its meaning must do proper *exegesis*. Meaning "to draw out," *exegesis* is the process of determining the original intent of Scripture by researching the language, culture, history, etc. of the biblical text. Fortunately, modern students of the Bible have access to well-researched commentaries that have done this necessary work for them.

How Eastern and Western thought differ

Over the past 35 years, I have identified more than two dozen significant differences in the Eastern and Western minds that shape people's perceptions of the intent of the original writers of the Bible.

[Topics are organized by similar content and not in order of importance]

EASTERN THOUGHT	WESTERN THOUGHT
Live in *time:* Values rest	Live in *space*: Always on the move

While shopping in a department store during a vacation visit to Hawaii—where many residents have been shaped by Eastern thought—my wife and I took our selections to a checkout counter where two salesladies were deep in conversation. They saw us standing there, but neither stopped talking to assist us. Eventually, they paused their discussion and rang up our sale.

This is characteristic behavior in many Eastern cultures. Time is something to enjoy. It's acceptable to move slowly, rest when necessary—even continue a conversation although there is work to do. There's little emphasis on punctuality.

In the West, however, it's considered disrespectful to arrive late to a meeting, appointment, work, or even social engagements where our sole intention is to have fun. That's because in the West, time is essential; it rules our lives. We constantly check our watch or phone for the time. We follow a to-do list as we complete our assignments throughout the day. Smartphones notify us when appointments draw near. Life in the West requires command of time and tools that measure it.

EASTERN THOUGHT	WESTERN THOUGHT
Emphasis on H*onor/Shame*: **Actions honor/shame family, tribe**	**Emphasis on *Right/Wrong*:** **Actions evaluated as good/bad**

The focus of Eastern cultures is the group. Relationships are necessary for life because life is found in the group. An individual's identity is tied directly to the group.

The family or tribe determines acceptable thoughts and behaviors for its members. If individuals violate these standards, they don't feel *personal* guilt. Rather, rule-breakers experience shame in the face of the family or tribe. The group alone ascribes shame; there is nothing individuals can do to remove it. Only the group has that power. Honor, too, is bestowed on individuals by the group based on their character, not their actions.

The West occupies a culture of right and wrong. Right and wrong are determined by laws that establish appropriate behavior within the culture. When individuals break a law, the consequences they suffer are dictated by the broken statute. The East's *honor and shame* are replaced in the West with *good and bad*. When individuals break the law, their bad character is exposed to society.

In the West, an individual's identity is largely determined by his or her achievements. It has little to do with the views of others. Reputation is largely created by individual achievements and has little to do with others' views. Education, job title, financial status, position in the group, and respect shown by others—all evidence one's view of self. Honor is given to the individual by society based on one's specific accomplishments. Right and wrong are determined by laws that establish appropriate behavior within the culture. When someone breaks a law, consequences are governed by the broken statute. Shame and honor are replaced with good and bad. When a law is broken, the bad character of the offender is exposed to society.

The contrast between Eastern honor/shame and Western right/wrong cultures has been exhibited through Muslim honor killings committed in the United States.

On New Year's Eve 2007, Yaser Said killed his daughters Amina and Sarah—ages 18 and 17—because he was unhappy that they were dating outside his Muslim faith. After shooting them both multiple times and leaving them in his taxi in front of the Omni Hotel in Irving, Texas, he avoided arrest for 12 years. Finally captured in 2020, Yaser Said was convicted on two counts of murder and sentenced to life in prison without the possibility of parole.[3]

Because he committed these murders in the United Stated, Yaser Said's actions were subject to U.S. law and its penalties (western culture). However, had he killed his daughters in his home country, he would not have been subject to arrest or prosecution, because honor killings are permissible in the United Arab Emirates (eastern culture).

Unfortunately, Muslim honor killings—in which families murder loved ones to eliminate the shame of a loved one's actions—have often been recorded in American history[4] and continue to occur.

EASTERN THOUGHT	WESTERN THOUGHT
Relationships transcend rules: Even when rules exist, family and tribe are more important	*Rules transcend relationships:* We are expected to follow rules, even at the expense of family and friends

Family is primary in Eastern cultures and extends to aunts, uncles, cousins, and even far-flung members of the clan. (It's not uncommon for me to encounter "cousins" of those I meet during visits to the Middle East). Family units often consist of multi-generational households.

During one visit to Israel, we were invited to meet the families of two brothers working at our East Jerusalem hotel. After a short drive, we arrived at a multi-story house and began our visit on the top floor, where we met the younger brother's wife and children. None of them could speak English, but they were honored that we had come to visit. After a cup of tea, we walked down to the next floor, where we repeated this scenario with the other brother's family. After walking down several more flights of stairs, we arrived at the home's ground floor, where Grandma and Grandpa lived. Again, we met them, enjoyed another cup of tea, and managed to visit, courtesy of the brothers' translations.

Eastern family units like these are very close. If a member of the family breaks an established rule—be it a civil or a family rule—the family, or even the extended tribe or clan, can excuse the offense, because their relationship with the offending family member is always more important than the rule.

In the West, family is important, but it's often fragmented. It's common for children to graduate from college and move to a city miles away from home to begin their first job. Marriage may further separate loved ones. Seldom does commitment to family cause adult children to stay close to their parents and raise a family of their own nearby. The arrival of grandchildren fractures families even more. Soon family members are scattered across a nation—or even the world.

Because Western cultures are committed to social rules and laws (above), families expect members who break the law to pay whatever price the law demands. The United States prides itself as a nation of laws, and Lady Justice guarantees "liberty and justice for all," regardless of family relationships. Lawbreakers may be relatives, but Western families expect them to face the consequences of their actions.

EASTERN THOUGHT	WESTERN THOUGHT
Passive: Like to contemplate	**Aggressive: Like to act**

In February 1942—roughly two months after the attack on Pearl Harbor—President Franklin Roosevelt issued Executive Order 9066, which authorized "the evacuation of all persons deemed a threat to national security from the West Coast to relocation centers further inland."[5] Translation: Japanese-Americans were a threat to their nation.

Among those relocated were my wife's parents and their families. Soon after Executive Order 9066 was penned, they were removed from their West Coast homes and taken to the Minidoka War Relocation Center in Magic Valley, Idaho, where they remained for the duration of the war, surrounded by barbed wire and armed guards in watchtowers.

These American citizens were incarcerated by their government without arrest, trial, or sentencing—but they didn't protest. When we asked Grandma "Why?" she said that they were sure the U.S. Government had their safety in mind. As a result, there was little thought of refusing the demand, even though many—including Cathy's family—lost everything when they were relocated. Their houses, businesses, and personal items were gone, but still, they accepted this new reality.

Their response to relocation exemplifies the passive temperament of the Eastern thinker: *Contemplate the situation and respond with dignity.*

A Western thinker's response would be very different. Recently, a draft of a U.S. Supreme Court majority opinion was leaked before it was officially announced by the court. Opponents of the opinion expressed their outrage by exercising their Constitutional right to publicly protest the decision of the majority justices. But some were so angry that they did not leave it at that: they protested in front of justices' private residences, an illegal act of aggression.

In Western thought, it's acceptable—even expected—to express disagreement with opposing views. In recent years, the hostility of such disagreements has escalated. Increasingly, the Western response to opposing ideas involves little contemplation or reflection, just immediate aggression, even if the point of contention is minor.

EASTERN THOUGHT	WESTERN THOUGHT
Accept the world as it is: Live in peace with nature	**Try to change the world/nature according to our desires; Impose our will on it**

Western culture is known to impose its will on nature by altering it for the perceived public good.

In the mid-1930s, the Tennessee Valley Authority (TVA) was created by the Roosevelt Administration to control flooding of the Tennessee River and provide hydroelectric power to residents and businesses located in the Tennessee Valley watershed.

Using the federal government's power of eminent domain[6] to obtain the 125,000 acres of privately owned land required for the project, the TVA displaced nearly 16,000 people in the process. Farms, crops, and entire villages were lost to the flooded Clinch River. Before just one of the project's 30 dams was completed to create Norris Lake, the small town of Loyston—all its homes, schools, businesses, churches, and cemeteries—had to be relocated.

The Pennsylvania Turnpike is another example of human will imposed on nature. Begun in 1880 but not finished until 1940, the Turnpike includes four-and-a-half miles of tunnels carved through the solid rock of seven mountains. This highway's existence is a tribute to Western thought: *If a mountain is in the way, simply tunnel through it.*

The Eastern mind tends to accept the world and nature as it finds them. Harmony with nature is viewed as a means to private peace. Walking through a wooded area, sitting by a mountain stream, or listening to a waterfall can bring calm and improve one's thinking ability. (It is interesting that vacationers in the West pay top dollar for a vacation room with a view of a mountain scene or a river valley.)

To the Eastern mind, nature is an opportunity for tranquility. Nature is viewed as a complement to human activity, not a challenge to it.

9

EASTERN THOUGHT	WESTERN THOUGHT
Future is determined by one's present good deeds	**Future is unknown; depends little on one's present good deeds**

During my senior year in college, I took a class that centered on Indian ethics and *karma*, the Eastern belief that one's future is determined by one's good or bad actions.

Yajnavalkya, an Indiana sage prominent in the development of the earliest Hindu texts, said, "According as one acts, according as one behaves, so does one become. The doer of good becomes good, the doer of evil becomes evil."[7]

The Old Testament presents a similar concept. One is expected to do good if a good outcome is desired. "Those who work their land will have abundant food, but those who chase fantasies have no sense (Proverbs 12:11)" Micah 6:8 describes what a good life pursues: "(God) has shown you, O mortal, what is good. And what does the LORD require of you? To act justly and to love mercy and to walk humbly with your God."

The Indian idea of karma leads to the concept of reincarnation. Future births and life situations are determined by actions done in one's present life, which itself was defined by the actions performed in previous lives. The Old Testament's result of living a good life contradicts that found in India but is still expressive of Eastern thinking: "For those who follow godly paths will rest in peace when they die (Isaiah 57:2)." Regardless of specific ethnic traditions, Eastern thought teaches that one's present actions affect one's future state.

Western societies tend to have a great deal of optimism about the future. They believe they can shape it through their actions. When the unexpected occurs, Western thinkers don't accept it calmly as Eastern thinkers do. Instead, they invest their efforts and resources in controlling its. impact on the future.

Western cultures are more creative in preparing for the future than Eastern societies. Western cultures invest in new and sometimes risky possibilities. Setting goals and planning steps to achieve them are part and parcel of the West's attempt to breach an unknown future.

They also invest in young people, whom they view as the future. When I was in college, a professor asked me where I saw myself in 10 years. This is a Western culture question.

EASTERN THOUGHT	WESTERN THOUGHT
Religion is the culture's first love: delight in pondering the meaning of life	**Science is the culture's first passion: delight in facts of physics**

Being Jewish can mean being part of a genetic group or adhering to a religious faith—or both. The origin of the race dates to Yahweh's encounter with a man named Abram that resulted in a covenant between them: God promised Abram—renamed *Abraham*—descendants more numerous than the sand on the seashore, a land where they could multiply, and the assurance that all the world's residents would be blessed through his family (Genesis 12 and 15).

Abraham's story continued through the lives of Isaac, Jacob, and Joseph. After 435 years[8] in Egypt (Exodus 12:40), the Israelites were led by Moses to Mount Sinai. There, Moses received 10 "laws" from God; four were designed to govern the Israelis' relationship with God; the other six related to their personal behavior. Referred to as the *Ten Commandments,* behavior became the foundation for the Torah, as well as for the expanded rules found in the Mishnah.[9]

In that Eastern culture, love for Yahweh (God) was expressed in love for Torah. Keeping the "Law" was how the Children of Israel conveyed their faithfulness to God. It was more important than anything else in life.

Similarly, observance of religious law—as defined by the Church based in Rome—was central to Western Christianity for centuries. So, too, was the fact that religion was more important than anything else in life. Art and architecture reflected this. Painters depicted biblical stories; churches and cathedrals were the largest structures in villages and cities.

However, all this changed during the 1500s in a cultural change called the Renaissance.

During the Renaissance, the Roman Church's works-based belief system was rejected by *Protest*ants. At the same time, the Church lost its iron grip on scientific knowledge, challenged by newly discovered writings of ancient Greek scholars that were making their way to Europe.

Freedom of thinking expanded, the views and absolute authority of the Church were questioned increasingly, and scientific discovery accelerated, it was a definite shift from Eastern to Western thinking.

This realignment of authority from religion to human reason was fully realized in the Enlightenment[10] of the 1700s. Advancements in literature, science—even religion—exploded. Medical practice today is the result of Enlightenment thinking. Medicine has advanced to the place where people assume doctors can correct or fix every physical ailment and are truly disappointed when they can't. Advances in mathematics and astronomy have permitted humans to walk on the moon and send a rover to investigate the surface of Mars.

In most Western cultures, faith in science and scientific research has replaced faith in Christ and His Church. Belief in God has declined. The Church is viewed by an increasing number of people as unnecessary, remote, and irrelevant.

EASTERN THOUGHT	WESTERN THOUGHT
Believe in the freedom of *silence*: **lapse into meditation**	**Believe in the freedom of** *speech*: **strive for articulation**

In Far Eastern cultures, *silence* means eliminating environmental noise *and* clearing one's mind of thoughts and distractions through the practice of meditation.

Meditation may be used to achieve inner peace, gain a greater awareness of oneself, or, as in Buddhism, attain enlightenment.

Biblical meditation is different. Scripture teaches that meditation is pondering a text with a receptive heart. Our receptivity allows God to teach us concepts about Scripture that we cannot grasp by simply reading it. Meditation requires us to "Be still and know that I am God" (Psalm 46:10) so that his Spirit can reveal truth to us.

"Being still" is easier said than done in Western culture. People in the West are uncomfortable with silence. When I walk into the family room, I automatically turn on the television. I seldom watch it or even know what program is on or what is being said, I simply want the background "noise." My wife says I'm the only person who wrote his entire doctoral dissertation while sitting in front of the TV.

"Noise" seems to be everywhere. Technology has created noise in nearly every environment we enter. Walk through any shopping mall in the West and most people you pass have earbuds or AirPods in their ears listening to a podcast or their favorite music. Sit in a doctor's office, and nearly everyone in the waiting room is staring at their cell phone (with their earbuds in).

Unlike the "silence" of Eastern cultures, the Western concept of Freedom of Speech created opportunities for *public speaking*. A hundred years ago this was conveyed by the Speakers' Corner in Hyde Park, London. This area provided open-air public speaking, debate, and discussion. Speakers articulated their arguments to convince audiences to accept their reasoning.

Eventually, several Speaker's Corners emerged in America. Cleveland, Berkeley, and Chicago, all provided public space for individual opinions to be shared with onlookers. Presently, the area of Pennsylvania Avenue on the north side of the White House has become a *de facto* Speaker's Corner. In fact, impromptu public speaking is legal in all public places in Washington DC.

Today, unfortunately, well-designed speeches and arguments have often been replaced by loud, angry shouts, and even rioting to express individual or group opinions.

Our vigorous exercise of the right to Freedom of Speech and advances in communications technology have created a Culture of Noise in the West.

Jobs, children, volunteering, exercise, and family activities demand most of our waking hours. Discovering time and a quiet place is difficult. To practice silence and biblical meditation requires intentional planning.

EASTERN THOUGHT	**WESTERN THOUGHT**
Marriage first, then love: marriage is the beginning of a love affair	**Love first, then marriage: marriage is the happy ending of a wonderful romance**

The musical *Fiddler on the Roof* depicts life in a Russian Jewish village before the Communist Revolution of 1917. It also presents both the Eastern and Western views of marriage.

Tevya, a poor milkman, is determined to find wealthy husbands for his daughters. As Jewish custom—anchored in Eastern thought—requires, Tevye consults the community matchmaker. His daughters, on the other hand, want to marry the young men with whom they are in love, a very Western idea. Trapped between the tradition of arranged marriage that had resulted in his marriage a quarter-century earlier and his daughters' yearnings, Teyve asks his wife Golde "Do you love me?"

> Golde replies, "For 25 years I've washed your clothes, cooked your meals, cleaned your house, given you children, milked the cow. After 25 years (you need to know) right now?"

> "But do you love me?" Tevya asks again, and she answers, "For 25 years I've lived with him, fought with him, starved with him. Twenty-five years my bed is his, if that's not love, what is?"

> "Then you love me?" Teyve asks. Golde's response? "I suppose I do."

Unlike Eastern couples, couples in the West freely develop their relationship *before* they commit to one another in marriage. But dating couples tend to be on their best behavior, so the relationship they develop may be based on false pretenses and result in surprises—usually unpleasant—after the ceremony. He sees her without makeup, she hears him belch, and they both realize the other has habits (and perhaps values) they had not revealed to each other when they were dating. Such surprises can destroy romance and challenge the hard work of building a relationship.

In Eastern culture, contact between couples is limited, highly regulated, or may not be permitted at all. Couples develop their relationship *after* they've married, free of the challenge of post-ceremony surprises.

EASTERN THOUGHT	WESTERN THOUGHT
Marriage is *arranged.*	Marriage is *self-determined.*

Eastern marriage is arranged by parents or other older family members, often without the knowledge of the bride and/or groom, sometimes even before they are born. Business agreements between the fathers may include the promise of marriage to a firstborn son or daughter.

For example, Jacob worked seven years for Rachel, but Laban substituted Leah on the wedding night. When confronted, Laban said, "It's not our custom here to marry off a younger daughter ahead of the firstborn (Genesis 29:26)." Rachel's father—not Rachel—had the final say on her marriage to Jacob and even had the authority to alter the original deal: Jacob had to work *another* seven years for Rachel.

In the West, young people start dating in their teens, with or without parental permission. They eventually decide if and who and when they want to marry. Although some consult their parents in the process, ultimately, they view these decisions as theirs alone to make. So does Western culture.

EASTERN THOUGHT	WESTERN THOUGHT
Marriage is an *indissoluble* covenant	Marriage is a *dissolvable* contract

In the East, marriage is an indissoluble covenant. This is the biblical position. Genesis 2:24 says, "a man leaves his father and mother and is joined to his wife, and the two are united into one." Jesus repeats this (Matthew 19:5; Mark 10:7) and it is restated by the Apostle Paul to the Ephesian church (Ephesians 5:31). My friend, Bob Stone, a family counselor, said that this joining is like gluing two pieces of paper together and then trying to separate them after the glue dries. You can't pull them apart without destroying both halves.[11]

When I was on a ministry trip to India in 1982, the staff of the country's Youth for Christ had to determine the future of a local staff person who had been unfaithful to his wife. Like many other Indian citizens, his was an arranged marriage. His wife not only disliked him; she detested his Christian faith. Upon learning of his infidelity, she called the Youth for Christ office and reported him.

The YFC staff had a decision to make: Could the man continue to serve as an evangelist to those young people with whom he had developed a relationship, or must he be removed due to his sin? Should their decision be influenced by the fact that he was in an arranged (aka forced) marriage where neither partner loved, respected, or cared for the other and lived in a culture where divorce was not permitted?

Although they were not without compassion for the man, they did not allow the circumstances of his marriage to muddy the biblical mandate: "You must not commit adultery," (Mt 19:18, Mk 10:19, Lk 18:20). They did the only thing they could: they released him from his position in the organization.

Marriage in the West is viewed as a dissolvable contract: "You keep your half of the contract and I'll keep mine. You break yours and I'm no longer committed to mine."

These contracts are created to protect one party from the actions of the other and can contain any terms to which both parties agree. My wife and I once attended a wedding at which the bride and groom committed themselves to each other "until our love ends"—which turned out to be about two years.

When marriage is viewed as a contract, it's always possible to find a way to break it. Courts in America accept the argument that couples have "irreconcilable differences." This means the parties are not willing to work on their disagreements. Social and broadcast media, movies, and the adult examples in their lives tell young people, "If it doesn't work out, just walk away."

The possibility that marriage contracts may be broken is inherent in their creation—and broken they are. The rate of divorce rate in the United States is among the highest in the world. As of this writing (2022), there are more than 750,000 divorces in our nation each year.[12]

In short, marriages in the West are designed to be broken.

EASTERN THOUGHT	WESTERN THOUGHT
Love is mute: try to conceal it from the world	**Love is vocal: delight in showing it to others**

In the West, it's acceptable for couples to express their love publicly by holding hands, kissing, hugging, touching, or cuddling. (More explicit public sexual expressions are considered unacceptable, although this, unfortunately, seems to be changing.) There is a biological reason for this. When couples are close, their bodies release oxytocin, the "cuddle" or "love hormone,"[13] which creates a feeling of calm and trust. Lips have high nerve sensitivity. This is partially why babies put things near or in their mouths to learn about their world. Kissing generates biological reactions that engender feelings of love.

Eastern people are inclined to conceal their romantic expressions. It's not that they have no sense of love or the desire to express it, but public displays of affection are not acceptable in their society. Unless the culture has been westernized, young and old alike avoid it.

Eastern suppression of love is not limited to public actions; it extends to words. Most spouses and family members never say the words, "I love you," even privately, to one another. (Remember Teyva and Golde above?). Most teenagers in Eastern cultures have never had their parents tell them in words that they are loved—but they also never doubt that they are. Eastern love is expressed and accepted through acts of love, not words or physical expressions.

What about the traditional kiss I receive from my Palestinian friends in Bethlehem each time I visit? This is a greeting, an expression of welcome conveyed by both women and men; it holds no romantic significance.

EASTERN THOUGHT	**WESTERN THOUGHT**
Self-denial is the secret of survival	**Self-assertiveness is key to success**

In Eastern cultures, there are two reasons to practice self-denial:

The *self* is defined by being a member of the group (see above). Self, therefore, has no identity outside the family, tribe, or clan. Self-denial exists for the sake of the group.

Religion. Deuteronomy 30:10 tells the Israelites "The LORD your God will delight in you if you obey his voice and keep the commands and decrees written in this Book of Instruction, and if you turn to the LORD your God with all your heart and soul." Faithful Jews must live in submission to Yahweh. Every aspect of life must be defined by obedience, submission, and dedication. This requires denying one's personal will and self and acquiring a *God-Self*. In the mind of the follower, his personal self stops existing and he becomes a disciple along with God's other disciples. "You must obey the LORD your God by keeping all these commands and decrees" (Deuteronomy 27:10).

In sharp contrast, Western societies encourage the development and defense of the *self*. The United States Constitution ensures its citizens certain individual rights. Self-assertiveness is the defensive reaction when one's rights, beliefs, or positions are challenged. This behavior doesn't have to be rude or offensive or even aggressive. It simply means there exists an inner knowledge that the self is important and has value. When that value is challenged, the natural reaction is to be assertive. Expressing oneself assertively can assist in standing for one's point of view and can be done while respecting the rights and beliefs of others. It also can boost one's self-esteem while earning others' respect.

Unfortunately, much self-assertiveness is not expressed this way. Challenges to one's point of view are often met with anger and hostility. Shouting, pushing, even fighting can result, and winning becomes the goal. This is no longer assertiveness, but aggression. Aggression is a "forceful action...intended to dominate or master"[14] another. It is the attempt to meet one's needs without regard for others' needs. Aggression invites an aggressive response—and the latter seldom results in understanding. The writer of Proverbs clearly describes the difference in outcomes between an assertive and aggressive response: "A gentle answer deflects anger, but harsh words make tempers flare" (15:1).

EASTERN THOUGHT	WESTERN THOUGHT
Taught to live simply on less and less	**Urged each day to gain more and more**

Poverty is widespread in many Middle Eastern countries and always has been. Even today, 20 percent of the Iraqi population live on $2 per day. Living on less and less has been a necessity since biblical times. The geography of the land required ancient residents to constantly move along the edges of the desert to find water and grass for their herds. There were few towns in antiquity and little money to purchase goods if there were. Residents lived nomadic lifestyles and lived on what they could make themselves or find on the land.

Perhaps you've seen the bumper sticker that reads, "He who dies with the most toys wins." In the West, especially in affluent communities, folks seem obsessed with owning "things." It is as if collecting items that bring fulfillment is one's goal in life. In my more than 30 years of youth ministry I routinely asked young people why they wanted to go to college, why they selected the profession they wanted to pursue, and what their life goals were after school. In nearly every instance I received the same answer: *I want to make lots of money!*

After their adult children leave home to begin life on their own, many parents sell the home where they raised their kids to move into a larger house. Cars, guns, boats, motorcycles, four-wheelers, travel vacations, vacation homes: all represent some of the many *toys* people collect.

In 2019, "over 30% of [American] households had an income exceeding $100,000 per year and over 30% of households had a net worth exceeding $250,000."[15] According to the U.S. Bureau of Labor Statistics, Americans spent over $3,000 per person on entertainment and recreation in 2019.[16] This is nearly four times what many in the Middle East make in a year. In 2018, Americans made an average of $78,000 and spent $61,000 [78%] of it.[17] Not all was spent on *toys*, but it's evidence that the average American household spends much of its annual income.

Is this affluent mindset wrong? Should we learn to live on less and less? Scripture does not say money is evil. It says the "love of money is the root of all kinds of evil" (1 Timothy 6:10). Morally, money itself is neither good nor bad. However, it does impact the attitude of people who spend it. The Apostle Paul says, "Everything is pure to those whose hearts are pure" (Titus 1:15). He goes on to say things become impure when "minds and consciences are corrupted."

Living in an affluent society is not wrong. Owning things is not wrong—unless our minds turn us from pure hearts to selfishly possessing things. Jesus told a parable about a farmer who continued to acquire more and more until his life was required of him and then he was asked, "who will get everything you worked for?" (Luke 12:16-21). The truth is, He who dies with the most toys doesn't win; he simply dies!

EASTERN THOUGHT	WESTERN THOUGHT
Love of life is the ideal	**Conquest (winning) is the ideal**

"Red" Sanders, UCLA football coach, is credited with telling his players, "Winning isn't everything — *long pause* — It's the only thing."[18] Unfortunately, that's the credo by which many in the West live their lives.

In sports, of course, winning is fun, but it's not the primary objective: the pursuit of excellence is. Its pursuit may or may not produce a win, but excellence will, however, create sportsmanship, discipline, fair play, integrity, character, respect for others, hard work, teamwork, and many other positive qualities. When winning replaces the pursuit of excellence as sport's ultimate goal, it produces blame, anger, and dirty play; it teaches players to be nasty, unfair, and unethical individuals.

In Eastern thinking, the meaning of life is centered on actions and thoughts of the family, tribe, or group one belongs to. Individual identity is found only in relation to the group; personal meaning and love of life are absorbed into identity with the group. People make decisions by consulting parents, elders, and others in the group. Group unity is the main point of one's life.

The Children of Israel was such a group: a confederation of tribes who descended from Abraham. "They are the people of Israel, chosen to be God's adopted children. God revealed his glory to them. He made covenants with them and gave them his law. He gave them the privilege of worshiping him and receiving his wonderful promises" (Romans 9:4). Identity within the Children of Israel was created by the unity of being a part of the group. Love of life was found in obeying the covenants that identified the group.

EASTERN THOUGHT	WESTERN THOUGHT
Glorifies austerity and sacrifice: poverty is an acceptable lifestyle	Emphasizes comfortable living and enjoyment of cultural status

Austerity is defined as a "situation in which there is not much money, and it is spent only on things that are necessary."[19]

By that definition, my 1950s childhood was austere. My parents' income was limited. My siblings and I always packed our lunches for school. We didn't have a TV or phone in our house until most of our friends had had them for years. However, my parents carefully managed their finances so we never lacked life's necessities. As kids we were happy, completely unaware that our standard of living was below "middle class." Looking back, I suspect we weren't living that far above the poverty line.

Today, many Western families live above the poverty level—but still are discontented. Although they have the basics of Western life—food, home ownership, adequate income—they are silently pushed to obtain more by the expectations of our consumer culture. This is especially true for young people. Eager to live up to the standards of the culture, they consider name-brand items superior to knock-offs, even though they cost much more.

Most people in Middle Eastern countries today live in a much inferior way to how I grew up in the 1950s. For example, currently,[20] 25 percent of West Bank Palestinians are unemployed; the unemployment rate among young men in their mid-20s—most with a wife and children—is nearly 30 percent.[21]

In the West Bank there's little possibility of escaping joblessness, so most of these young men and their families live simply, purchasing only absolute necessities. Western values appeal to them but there seems to be no escape. Hamas exploits this situation by offering young unemployed men a lifetime annual salary for their families if they martyr themselves by attacking Israelis. Those who refuse martyrdom continue their struggle with poverty.

Untouched by modern affluence, poverty was the norm in ancient Israel. Scripture says those living in poverty were close to God's heart.[22] The poor were said to be blessed[23] and instructed to value integrity over riches.[24] In ancient Israel it was never expected that the poor would become rich ("There will always be some in the land who are poor" Dt 15:11). A lifestyle of poverty was a reality for most citizens, both the Children of Israel and foreigners in their land. The few rich among them were commanded to care for the poor and widows.[25]

To live in continual poverty can lead to the development of a society permanently adapted to that reality. This is called a "culture of poverty."[26] Once this attitude becomes an accepted lifestyle, living in poverty becomes not only acceptable but expected. This is how life was lived during much of ancient Israel's history. The reality of a life destined for poverty created a culture of poverty among the people. But this was not limited to ancient times. It exists in many third-world traditions today.

Such a cultural attitude is very difficult to correct, even in today's global environment with the influence of western affluence. "Many countries ...seem incapable of helping themselves. They have reached the point where outside aid tends to do more to prolong problems than solve them."[27] When poverty becomes an accepted lifestyle, escape is difficult even when western culture allures people to join it.

EASTERN THOUGHT	WESTERN THOUGHT
Timeliness: awareness of events happening on time; as God planned.	*Time-Oriented*: checking watch, schedule, calendar; being on time for event

To Western-minded Americans, time is money, a limited commodity, and therefore priceless. Time is fleeting; it moves rapidly. Therefore, time must be managed properly for our benefit.

The Apostle Paul's letter to the Ephesians reflects this point of view: "Be careful how you live. Don't live like fools, but like those who are wise. Make the most of every opportunity" (5:15-16).

To avoid wasting time, we in the West have become conscious of how we use it. Alarms wake us in the morning. In school, bells signal when to change classes; factory whistles tell us when to change shifts and take breaks. This seems so logical to us—so normal—that it comes as a surprise to discover that in other parts of the world, people have a very different concept of time.

In the East, there is no such concept as wasted time or not being on time. The Eastern mind believes that time will be there again tomorrow and the next day, and the next. Each day will create its own opportunities, risks, and dangers. There is no rush to address problems or make decisions about important things. Other days will come when decisions can be made. Clocks, watches, and smartphones cannot alter one's judgment. Meetings can easily be moved to another time if family obligations interfere.

In Eastern thinking, plans aren't important because time cannot be controlled or managed to produce the desired outcome. Proverbs 16:9 confirms this: "We can make our plans, but the LORD determines our steps." God has control of life's major events and will cause them to happen in their proper time; they do not require human participation.

EASTERN THOUGHT	WESTERN THOUGHT
Think corporately/ collectively: family, community, society (People of God). People are connected; duty to one another is mandatory.	Think individually: individual rights (personal relationship with Christ). Human beings are independent operators in the universe and society.

The Eastern mind thinks *corporately* or *collectively*. When Eastern thinkers confront problems, their commitment to family/tribe/community is the primary factor in their decisions and actions.

The Western mind thinks in terms of the *individual and personal rights*. Because the Constitution guarantees Americans personal rights, we tend to view every situation in terms of our civil liberties. We even speak of our salvation as a personal thing: *I have a personal relationship with Jesus.* We accept him as our "personal" savior.

However, the Bible—reflecting Eastern thinking—describes salvation in corporate/collective terms: "But to all who believed him and accepted him, he gave the right to become *children of God* (John 1:12).

So, is it wrong to say, "I have accepted Jesus as my *personal* savior"? Of course not, as long as we understand that we are merely expressing the desire to start a relationship with Him as part of a collective group, the *Children of God.*

According to Romans 8:14, the *Children of God* are those who are led by His Spirit, not those who "make a decision." Reciting a prayer of commitment does not make us God's children: it simply signals that we trust Jesus to forgive us and intend to obey him in daily life. We cannot do the latter without being led by the Spirit of God, and we cannot be led by the Spirit without a relationship with God. That relationship makes us "people of God."

EASTERN THOUGHT	WESTERN THOUGHT
Cherish wisdom that comes with age	**Cherish vitality of youth**

After Moses received the Law at Sinai (Exodus 24), the Lord told him to invite 70 of Israel's elders to join in experiencing Him more intimately than the rest of Israel. Beginning with this event and throughout both Old and New Testament times, elders were an important part of Israel's future.

Unlike the position of "elder" found in today's Christian church, elders in ancient Israel were older men selected to represent the people and preside over their religious and civil issues. When trouble arose, the elders met at the city gate where they held court. In true Eastern tradition, it was believed that these older men had the experience and wisdom they could use to govern Israel. By the time Jesus was teaching, these elders had become the 70-member ruling council known as the Sanhedrin.

In today's Eastern cultures, elders of the family, tribe, and clan are still accorded the highest degree of love and respect. Younger people consider them an inspiration.

In the West, we instead revere the vitality of youth. We place great value on the physical strength of young men and women because it helps them accomplish things. They also bring an eagerness to every activity they pursue.

Western thinkers recognize that there may be value in honoring the wisdom of older folks, but they also know that advancing age doesn't automatically make people kinder, more giving, or better men or women. If Western thinkers look to older members of their family, tribe, or clan for wise counsel, it's because their elders have already proved they can provide it.

EASTERN THOUGHT	WESTERN THOUGHT
In old age, enjoy one's extended family	**In old age, enjoy the fruits of one's labor**

Eastern culture respects its elders and embraces the duty of caring for them in old age. God's fifth commandment requires this: "Honor your father and mother" (Exodus 20:12). Households typically consist of intergenerational extended families, including grandparents, children, grandchildren, and often aunts, uncles, and cousins.

When I asked the owner of a Nazareth restaurant if the locals frequent his shop in the evenings, he said, "I close after lunch so I can be home when my grandchildren arrive after school." Living with extended family allows elders to enjoy younger members and watch them grow; often, elders are expected to help care for children while younger adults work outside the home. As elders grow even older, younger family members provide care so they can continue to live at home. Often, they die at home, surrounded by loved ones who mourn together. Elders are usually buried within hours of their death in a location that permits the family to visit often.

It's quite different in Western culture.

Adult children may move hundreds of miles from their parents to pursue their careers, then sink roots in their new community and establish a family there. Frequent, in-person contact between elders and younger family members are replaced by phone calls and virtual visits. Many elders never see their grandchildren grow through elementary and senior high school.

As they approach retirement, elders feel free to plan their future apart from extended family members who have chosen to live far away. Retirees who live in cold climes may relocate to warmer ones; relocation means leaving only friends, church, and community.

Because many elders have no one living nearby to care for them as they age, they tend to live their later years in senior communities, assisted-living facilities, or skilled nursing homes. They grow older with their peers, apart from family. When death comes, they may not be surrounded by family. They may have even preplanned their funeral without family involvement, arranging for burial in a cemetery miles removed from family, who will seldom return to visit their graves.

No wonder as we travel the freeway, we see the bumper sticker on the back of a motor home that reads, "We're spending our children's inheritance."

EASTERN THOUGHT	WESTERN THOUGHT
Think concretely: pragmatically, functionally	**Think abstractly: metaphysically (nature of being and the world)**

Western minds read the ancient Hebrew text of the Bible with their Greco-Roman mindset. The irony is that the Hebrew text was written by Eastern thinkers who lived *before* the Greco-Roman period.

The Western (Greek) mind thinks "metaphysically (μετὰ τὰ φυσικά)," i.e., *after or beyond or above the physical world.* To think metaphysically is to think about abstract concepts like "the fundamental nature of reality, the first principles of being, identity and change, space and time, causality, truth. It is the attempt to answer the questions: 'What is there? and What is it like?'"[28]

The Western mind also thinks *visually*, i.e., what does something look like? We ask questions like, "What did Jesus look like?" or "What did a city gate look like?"

Greek architecture reflects this mindset, too. Form, structure, and appearance are most important. Rather than construct a perfectly functional-but-square building—*Boring!*—Greeks focused on creating a building with proportions that were pleasing to the eye. They tapered columns to make them look taller. When they realized that the perfectly straight outer columns of the Parthenon would appear to lean outward, they leaned them slightly inward. They also built the Parthenon's floor higher at its center than at its edges so it didn't look as if it sagged in the middle.

In contrast, an Eastern (Middle Eastern) mind thinks "functionally." Rather than words that convey structure or form, their descriptions convey a deeper meaning. They suggest what things *do* and what they *are for*. This is biblical imagery.

The <u>Wittenburg Door</u>[29] once printed a drawing to capture the "beauty" of the writer's lover as described in the Eastern biblical imagery of the Song of Solomon 4:1-7:

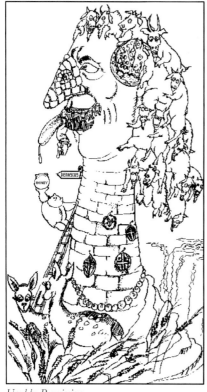

Used by Permission

"How beautiful you are, my darling! Oh, how beautiful! Your eyes behind your veil are doves. Your hair is like a flock of goats descending from Mount Gilead. Your teeth are like a flock of sheep just shorn, coming up from the washing. Each has its twin; not one of them is alone. Your lips are like a scarlet ribbon; your mouth is lovely. Your temples behind your veil are like the halves of a pomegranate. Your neck is like the tower of David, built with elegance; on it hang a thousand shields, all of them shields of warriors. Your two breasts are like two fawns, like twin fawns of a gazelle that browse among the lilies. Until the day breaks and the shadows flee, I will go to the mountain of myrrh and to the hill of incense. All beautiful you are, my darling; there is no flaw in you."

EASTERN THOUGHT	WESTERN THOUGHT
Convey truthful stories: more philosophical; need not be proven	**Convey scientific truth: facts proven through the scientific method and experimentation**

A miracle is an act of God that transcends the natural order. Scripture contains many such events:

> Joshua 10:12-13 "[12] On the day the LORD gave the Israelites victory over the Amorites, Joshua prayed to the LORD in front of all the people of Israel. He said, 'Let the sun stand still over Gibeon, and the moon over the valley of Aijalon.' [13] So the sun stood still and the moon stayed in place until the nation of Israel had defeated its enemies."

> Exodus 14:21-22 "[21] Then Moses raised his hand over the sea, and the LORD opened up a path through the water with a strong east wind. The wind blew all that night, turning the seabed into dry land. [22] So the people of Israel walked through the middle of the sea on dry ground, with walls of water on each side!"

> Matthew 15:32-39 "[35] So Jesus told all the people to sit down on the ground. [36] Then he took the seven loaves and the fish, thanked God for them, and broke them into pieces. He gave them to the disciples, who distributed the food to the crowd. [37] They all ate as much as they wanted. Afterward, the disciples picked up seven large baskets of leftover food."

> Luke 7:12 & 14 "[12] A funeral procession was coming out as he approached the village gate. The young man who had died was a widow's only son, and a large crowd from the village was with her...[14] Then he walked over to the coffin and touched it, and the bearers stopped. "Young man," he said, "I tell you, get up." [15] Then the dead boy sat up and began to talk! And Jesus gave him back to his mother.

Western thinking—especially since the Enlightenment—rests on the scientific principle that the supernatural cannot exist. Most folks in the West—skeptics and many Christians alike—reject the Bible because of its miraculous tales. Thomas Jefferson, the third President of the United States, sat at his desk in the White House one evening and, using two copies of the Bible, began cutting the sections he agreed with and pasting them to a blank journal. The parts he didn't accept—walking on water, miracles, virgin birth, resurrection, etc.—he left dangling in the two mutilated books.[30] A printed copy of the Jefferson Bible now resides in the Smithsonian's Museum of American History. Most Church members today are not as brash as Jefferson. Rather than "cut and paste," they simply ignore scriptures they don't believe.

What is the difference between believing these miraculous stories and refusing to believe? It is the difference between true and truth.

When we say something is *true*, we are saying it is *real, accurate,* or *factually correct*.

A fact is something that's indisputable, based on empirical research and quantifiable measures. Facts go beyond theories. They're proven through calculation and experience, or they're something that definitively occurred in the past.

Truth is entirely different; it may include fact, but it can also include belief. Oftentimes, people will accept things as true because they fall closer to their comfort zones, are assimilated easily into their comfort zones, or reflect their preconceived notions of reality. Fact is indisputable. Truth is acceptable.[31]

The Eastern mind does not insist that stories of miracles be proven factually. They believe them based on the stories themselves. Their belief that God—who created the natural—can perform the supernatural is all that is needed to move the story into the realm of the real. Even if the facts of the story cannot be proven, the truth(s) it teaches can be merged into their belief system.

EASTERN THOUGHT	WESTERN THOUGHT
Characterized by mystery	Characterized by the bottom line: the lowest common denominator

Scripture contains many references to mystery (Hb, רָזָה - Gk, μυστήριον). A *mystery* is a secret or hidden reality that cannot be known without a revelation from God.

The Old Testament—the Hebrew Bible of Eastern minds—contains many references to God's secret plans. For example, Proverbs 25:2 says, "It is God's privilege to conceal things." Deuteronomy 29:29 reveals that "The LORD our God has secrets known to no one." However, God promises to disclose these when appropriate: "Ask me and I will tell you remarkable secrets you do not know about things to come" (Jeremiah 29:29).

Isaiah 11 talks about a mystery that the Israelites were eager for God to reveal: "Out of the stump of David's family will grow a shoot—yes, a new Branch bearing fruit from the old root. And the Spirit of the LORD will rest on him—the Spirit of wisdom and understanding, the Spirit of counsel and might, the Spirit of knowledge and the fear of the LORD" (vv 1-2).

Over the centuries, Israel evolved with this expectation of God's coming Messiah. Anticipation grew through a period of *theocracy* (God rule), *monarchy* (king rule), and *dispersion* among the nations (dominant rule). Even today, under *self rule,* faithful Jews await the coming of their Messiah.

In his letter to the Ephesian church, the Apostle Paul revealed the mystery of this long-awaited redeemer of the Jewish nation: "that is, the mystery made known to me by revelation... which was not made known to people in other generations... And this is God's plan: Both Gentiles and Jews who believe the Good News share equally in the riches inherited by God's children. Both are part of the same body, and both enjoy the promise of blessings because they belong to Christ Jesus (3:3-6)." Paul presented Jesus as the fulfillment of this long-awaited ruler.

In the Colossian epistle, Paul stated, "the mystery that has been kept hidden for ages and generations but is now disclosed to the Lord's people. To them God has chosen the glorious riches of this mystery, which is Christ in you, the hope of glory" (1:26-27). Paul revealed the mystery that the Israelites failed to believe: "I do not want you to be ignorant of this mystery, brothers and sisters, so that you may not be conceited: Israel has experienced a hardening in part until the full number of the Gentiles has come in, and in this way all Israel will be saved. As it is written: 'The deliverer will come from Zion: he will turn godlessness away from Jacob. And this is my covenant with them when I take away their sins'" (Romans 11:25-27). Israel's redeemer is also the Gentile's redeemer. God has welcomed the Gentiles by adopting[32] them into the kingdom of Jesus along with his Jewish brothers and sisters.

In contrast, Western thinking eschews mystery and centers on the bottom line, i.e., "the essential or salient point; the primary or most important consideration."[33] In math it's called the least common denominator,[34] but the least common denominator isn't limited to mathematics. When I was in college doing itinerate evangelism, I coined the term *Ingrown Eyeballs*. This is when we ask, "What will it cost me?" "What do I get from it?" "Will it benefit me?" "Will anyone see me?" Ingrown eyeballs can affect our decisions—even preventing us from making decisions that are essential.

When I evaluate everything only as it relates to me, I am concerned with the bottom line, the least common denominator: *Me*. When I think only of myself, I fail to fulfill the responsibilities God has required of me in treating others:[35] loving, serving, being kind, being hospitable, encouraging, etc. The Apostle Paul warns us to not "think you are better than you really are. Be honest in your evaluation" (Romans 12:3).

EASTERN THOUGHT	**WESTERN THOUGHT**
Views history as linear. God participates in history with His people.	Views history as cyclical. The forces that induce human action repeat.

The Eastern linear view of history is foundational to Judaism and the texts of the Hebrew Bible. For example, Creation was not cyclical, but sequential, with God acting day by day. Linear history is dominant in the Torah and Jewish thought. The Hebrew Bible—what Christians call the *Old Testament*—includes many instances in which the Israelites hold feasts or create stacks of stone to memorialize and celebrate God's participation with them in their linear history.

In the West, the change of seasons, day and night, good times and bad times, all express cycles. The Western mind views its history as cyclical, too, believing that the major forces that influence human actions—religion, politics, science, philosophy, and morality—occur in cycles.

For example, Westerners believe that Christianity peaked at the end of three different cycles in history: 1) in the 2nd century A.D., when believers gained political power; 2) in the Middle Ages, when church control over society expanded, but the spiritual life of church leadership waned; and 3) during the Reformation, when the Faith split into many branches, each renewing itself into a distinctive body.

Cyclical thinking has enormous implications. Whatever a society does during one cycle will change or even be erased in the next cycle. Western thinkers may view actions in their lifetime as valuable to them and their future while realizing those actions may eventually be replaced by others with completely opposite results.

EASTERN THOUGHT	WESTERN THOUGHT
God is good and is aware of one's situation. The purpose of prayer, then, is not to ask God to change our circumstances but to align our will with the situation He has given.	God is good and aware of our circumstances. The purpose of prayer is to ask God to intervene, changing both His will and our circumstances.

Deuteronomy 11:13 says "if you love the LORD your God and serve him with all your heart."

How do we serve God with our whole heart? Through prayer.

Following the Babylonian Exile, as Hebrew was spoken less and less, written prayers were created. Scholarship suggests that beginning in the Second Temple Period (Herod the Great and Jesus), prayer appeared as "liturgical formulations of a communal nature designated for particular occasions and conducted in a center totally independent of Jerusalem and the Temple, making use of terminology and theological concepts that were later to become dominant in Jewish and, in some cases, Christian prayer."[36]

The Hebrew root word for prayer is *palal* (פלל), which means "to judge." In the Eastern-minded Jewish tradition, prayer, then, is "judging oneself" with the goal of transformation. Jewish prayer is seldom a spontaneous discussion with God, but the recitation of ancient traditional written (and sometimes memorized) praises and thanks to Him.

In Judaism, praying communally—with others—is the norm, but individual prayer is not prohibited. Rarely do Jews who pray individually ask God for personal favors, although they may ask for strength to face challenges, forgiveness for personal imperfections, or help in living a better life.

The written prayers of Judaism ask God to benefit all Jews and humankind in general, e.g., bring peace on Earth, comfort those who mourn, free the captive, and support the Jewish people. Jewish prayers express the hopes, dreams, and values of all Jews, and reinforce their determination to better themselves and the world around them.

Jewish (Eastern thought) prayer does not attempt to influence God to change a situation; instead, it asks for God's help in accepting it. In contrast, it is not uncommon for Christians in the West to ask God to change or eliminate pain, discord, or disease—even death.

Is it wrong to ask God for healing or to correct an injustice? Of course not! The result of prayer, however, must be in line with God's will, not ours. (Think of Jesus' praying in Gethsemane: Mt 26:39).

Does God heal today? Of course!

I have a friend who had COVID-19 and was at the point of death; God healed him instantaneously, his 104° fever dropping to normal in four seconds. My friend, who is a physician, sat straight up and proclaimed, "He told me it is not my time yet!" His daughter and wife, who is a nurse, witnessed this miracle. However, God never promised that all will be healed. I lost another close friend to the COVID-19 virus, although many people had prayed for her healing.

Praying for God's intervention in life's circumstances is not only acceptable but expected. The Apostle Paul told the Philippian church to "pray about everything. Tell God what you need and thank him for all he has done" (4:6-7). Our needs/circumstances are important to God, but we tread on dangerous territory when we demand His intervention. God is our Master, and we serve Him; we must not reverse roles by expecting Him to act as a servant who should supply our needs, heal us, and/or change our circumstances.

A misinterpretation of Isaiah 53:5 ("by his stripes we are healed") can lead to false prayer. Isaiah was writing to Israel during their captivity in Babylon. The question in every Hebrew mind was, "Why would God permit this suffering when we were faithful in following his sacrificial commands?"

"By his stripes" referred to the salvation the coming Messiah would provide through his death scenario: beating, lashing, and crucifixion. Isaiah was predicting that salvation would replace the sacrifices that ceased when the Temple was destroyed. When we read Isaiah 53:5 today, we think it refers to our present need for physical healing, but it actually addressed Israel's need for *spiritual* healing.

EASTERN THOUGHT	WESTERN THOUGHT
God is like what God has done; anything more is idolatry	**God is known through systematic theology**

The Ancient Greeks thought their gods existed in corporeal form in the *Pantheon,* a world of gods high above the physical world. (Although these gods could make themselves invisible or transform themselves into animals or other beings, their default form was that of a human). As a result, the Greek-inspired Western mind tends to view God from a human perspective, describing Him in human terms: He is a *father.* He has a *son.* We refer to His hands, His eyes, His arms. We use the same pronouns to refer to Him that we use for men: *He, His, Him.*

Nearly every Western pastor who has attended a theological seminary in this country has been taught about God through *Systematic Theology,* "an orderly, rational, and coherent account of the doctrines of the Christian faith. It addresses issues such as what the Bible teaches about certain topics or what is true about God and His universe."[37]

Students of systematic theology begin with Genesis 1:1 and read through Revelation 22:21. Every time they find a statement about God, they record it in their notes in the "God column." They repeat this process for every theological concept in the Bible: *Jesus, Holy Spirit, Church, Humans, Sin, Salvation, etc.* When they complete the entire process, students investigate each column to discover truths about its topic.

For example, a student will learn that there are four aspects of God's nature, or *essence: God is Spirit, God is Self-Existent, God is Eternal, and God is Trinity (unified).* In addition to His essence, God possesses nine attributes or qualities that describe His being: omniscience (all-knowing), omnipotence (all powerful), omnipresence (present everywhere), immutability (unchanging), holiness, truth, love, mercy, and patience.

None of these concepts are found in Scripture because ancient Hebrews did not think this way.

The Hebrew writers described God in terms of relationship. Biblical language uses two constructs: subject and object. God is the *subject* of the universe, the Creator who began everything and will eventually end it. Humanity and material things are created beings and thus *objects*.

To the Eastern mind, human understanding of God begins at the point of contact between the *subject* and *object*. God as *revelatory*. In other words, He reveals Himself when it's necessary, e.g., *At that moment the Spirit of the LORD came powerfully upon him [Sampson] (Judges 14:6).*

The Old Testament tells us that the Hebrew people set up memorials to mark those moments when God met them in relationship and participated with them in personal experiences.

For the ancient Hebrew,[38] then, it is simple: *God is like what he has done.* He can be expected to treat humans as He has in the past.

Conclusion

We cannot divorce ourselves from who we are or how we think.

Both the Old and New Testaments reflect Eastern thinking, and we must keep that in mind in our reading and interpretation of Scripture.

Abdu Murray, co-author of <u>Seeing Jesus from the East</u>,[39] challenges us with this:

> *Jesus is authentically Eastern, but he's also authentically transcultural. He breaches all the nationalistic and ethnic borders that we have in place for him, and he belongs to no one, but he belongs to everyone, and he speaks everyone's language...he is arguably history's most influential figure. No one can really argue that point. And if he's the most influential figure of all time, then it's important for everyone, Western, Eastern, Southern, and Northern to understand the context he worked in to see the richness of his ministry and the impact on history."*[40]

As we read the Gospels and ponder what Jesus taught, we must remember that He was a first-century, Middle Eastern, Palestinian-thinking Jew. Otherwise, we cannot truly understand His teachings.

Notes

1 The Ballad of East and West. The Kipling Society. https://www.kiplingsociety.co.uk/poem/poems_eastwest.htm

2 Richard E. Nisbett (April 5, 2003). The Geography of Thought: How Asians and Westerners Think Differently...and Why. New York, NY: Free Press. p 89.

3 Rebecca Lopez (February 21, 2022). He's accused in the 'honor killings' of his daughters. Now, we're hearing from him first-hand in letters to judge. WFAA 8 ABC. https://www.wfaa.com/article/news/local/yaser-said-suspected-honor-killings-writes-letters-judge/287-ac817b72-f3ca-49d7-9013-fc7953cac698

4 Tina Isa was a normal 16-year-old, an honors student, giggling with her friends over cute boys, enjoying teen music, and working at Wendy's. But on November 6, 1989, Tina Isa was murdered by her parents in St. Louis, Missouri, in an honor killing. "Die! Die quickly!...Die, my daughter, die!" her father cried as he plunged a butcher knife six times into the breast of his daughter. Zein and Maria Isa were found guilty of the killing and sentenced to death. Both died while in prison. [DAVID J. KRAJICEK (Nov 10, 2013). Justice Story: 'Die, my daughter, die!' An old-world 'honor killing' in modern St. Louis. New York Daily News. https://www.nydailynews.com/news/justice-story/justice-story-honor-killing-article-1.1510125]

In May 2011 Rahim Alfetlawi, a Minnesota man, murdered his stepdaughter for not being Muslim enough. He was charged with first degree murder. [Police: Man Killed Stepdaughter For Not Following Islam (May 4, 2011). 62CBS Detroit. https://detroit.cbslocal.com/2011/05/04/man-accused-of-killing-stepdaughter-for-not-following-islam/]

Nada Huranieh was murdered on August 21, 2017, by her 16-year-old son who, encouraged by his father, suffocated his mother and threw her body out a second story window. The father had convinced his son that their divorce was the result of his wife's rejecting the traditional Syrian Islamic customs by not wearing a hijab and her permissive parenting of their two daughters, ages 12 and 14. Muhammad Alantawi was found guilty first-degree premeditated murder and was sentenced to life in prison without parole. [Mike Martindale (September 14, 2017). 'Americanized' kids riled dad; matricide suspected. The Detroit News. https://www.detroitnews.com/story/news/local/oakland-county/2017/09/14/farmington-hills-mom-dies-fall/105618994/; follow up, March 14, 2022, Farmington Hills man found guilty of first-degree murder of his mother https://www.detroitnews.com/story/news/local/oakland-county/2022/03/14/farmington-hills-man-found-guilty-first-degree-murder-his-mother/7040938001/]

Noor Almaleki refused to be her father's puppet. She was determined to live how she wanted, and did. Noor's father was enraged by this behavior. He believed, "a man's daughters are his property, and they are supposed to live with him until he decides otherwise." Females who rejected this position were considered guilty of dishonoring their family and clan. To an Iraqi there's nothing worse. So, Faleh Almaleki drove his jeep SUV into Noor and a friend while crossing a parking lot in Phoenix, Arizona. Doctors announced Noor clinically brain dead on November 2, 2009. Her heart stopped beating when she was removed from life support. Faleh Almaleki was sentenced to 34 years in prison for the assault. [Paul Rubin (March 31, 2010). Honor Thy Father: A Muslim man in Phoenix "honor killed" his American daughter. RiverFront Times. https://www.riverfronttimes.com/news/honor-thy-father-a-muslim-man-in-phoenix-honor-killed-his-americanized-daughter-2492622]

5   Executive Order 9066. National Archives. https://www.archives.gov/historical-docs/todays-doc/?dod-date=219

6   Eminent domain permits the government to take privately owned land for public use if owners are properly compensated.

7   Yajnavalkya. Britannica.
https://www.britannica.com/biography/Yajnavalkya

8   See: David Glatt-Gilad, How Many Years Were the Israelites in Egypt? The Torah.com. https://www.thetorah.com/article/how-many-years-were-the-israelites-in-egypt; David Wright (July 5, 2010). How Long Were the Israelites in Egypt? Answers in Genesis. https://answersingenesis.org/bible-questions/how-long-were-the-israelites-in-egypt/; Robert Carter and Lita Sanders (Sept 21, 2021). How long were the Israelites in Egypt? Creation.com. https://creation.com/how-long-were-the-israelites-in-egypt

9   written collection of the Jewish oral traditions

10 An "intellectual movement of the 17th–18th century in which ideas concerning God, reason, nature, and man were blended into a worldview that inspired revolutionary developments in art, philosophy, and politics. Central to Enlightenment thought were the use and celebration of reason." Encyclopedia Britannica. https://www.britannica.com/summary/Enlightenment-European-history

11 Bob Stone. Family Life Conference. Findlay, Ohio

12 Branka Vuleta (January 28, 2021). Divorce Rate in America [35 Stunning Stats for 2022]. Legaljobs. https://legaljobs.io/blog/divorce-rate-in-america/

13 Oxytocin. Psychology Today. https://www.psychologytoday.com/us/basics/oxytocin

14 Aggression. Merriam-Webster Dictionary. https://www.merriam-webster.com/dictionary/aggression

15 Affluence in the United States. Wikipedia. https://en.wikipedia.org/wiki/Affluence_in_the_United_States

16 Kristen May (July 2, 2021). How Much Should Someone Budget for Entertainment? Sapling. https://www.sapling.com/12144197/much-should-someone-budget-entertainment

17 Lexington Law (January 6, 2020). American Spending Habits in 2020. https://www.lexingtonlaw.com/blog/credit-cards/american-spending-habits.html

18 Winning isn't everything, it's the only thing. Wikipedia. https://en.wikipedia.org/wiki/Winning_isn%27t_everything;_it%27s_the_only_thing

19 Austerity. The Britannica Dictionary. https://www.britannica.com/dictionary/austerity

20 This was written in 2022

21 Youth Unemployment Rate for Developing Countries in Middle East and North Africa (February 16, 2022). FRED. Economic Research. https://fred.stlouisfed.org/series/SLUEM1524ZSMNA

22 Psalm 140:12 (NIV) "the **LORD** secures justice for the poor and upholds the cause of the needy."
Proverbs 14:31 (NIV) "Whoever oppresses the poor shows contempt for their Maker, but whoever is kind to the needy honors God."

23 Luke 6:20 (NIV) "Blessed are you who are poor, for yours is the kingdom of God."

24 Proverbs 28:6 (ESV) "Better is a poor man who walks in his integrity than a rich man who is crooked in his ways."

25 Deuteronomy 15:7-10 (NIV) "[7] if there are any poor Israelites in your towns when you arrive in the land the LORD your God is giving you, do not be hard-hearted or tightfisted toward them...[10] Give generously to the poor, not grudgingly, for the LORD your God will bless you in everything you do."

26 Created by the anthropologist Oscar Lewis in his 1959 book, *Five Families: Mexican Case Studies in the Culture of Poverty*, the culture of poverty theory states that living in pervasive poverty leads to a culture adapted to those conditions. Reprint: Basic Books (December 11, 1975). Critics of Lewis' theory present modern

arguments against it but ancient peoples were trapped within a lifestyle of poverty that created within them a justification for their plight.

27 Anthony H. Cordesman (August 24, 2020). The Greater Middle East: From the "Arab Spring" to the "Axis of Failed States." Center for Strategic & International Studies. https://www.csis.org/analysis/greater-middle-east-arab-spring-axis-failed-states

28 Metaphysics. Wikipedia. https://en.wikipedia.org/wiki/Metaphysics

29 Christian satire and humor magazine, published by the non-profit Trinity Foundation in Dallas, Texas. The magazine started publication in 1971 and ceased publication in 2008. Returned online publication in 2020, www.wittenburgdoor.com. Drawing used by Permission: NOVEMBER/DECEMBER 1990 ISSUE #114, pg 37 by Den Hart, Courtesy The Wittenburg Door.

30 Peter Carlson (September 27, 2017). The Bible According to Thomas Jefferson. Historynet. https://www.historynet.com/bible-according-thomas-jefferson/

31 Larry Walsh. Two Realities: Truth and Fact (and They're Not the Same). Channelnomics. https://channelnomics.com/2018/03/two-realities-truth-and-fact-and-theyre-not-the-same/

32 Ephesians 1:4-6 - "[4] For he chose us in him before the creation of the world to be holy and blameless in his sight. In love [5] he predestined us for adoption to sonship through Jesus Christ, in accordance with his pleasure and will— [6] to the praise of his glorious grace, which he has freely given us in the One he loves."

33 Bottom Line. Merriam-Webster Dictionary. https://www.merriam-webster.com/dictionary/bottom%20line

34 "the smallest number that can be used for all denominators of two or more fractions." Least Common Denominator.

https://www.mathsisfun.com/definitions/least-common-denominator.html

35 Loving others (John 13:34-35), Serving others (Galatians 5:13), Being kind to others (1 Thessalonians 5:15), Being hospitable to others (1 Peter 4:9), Encouraging others (1 Thessalonians 4:18)

36 Reif, Stefan C. (19–23 January 2000). "The Second Temple Period, Qumran Research and Rabbinic Liturgy: Some Contextual and Linguistic Comparisons". Fifth Orion International Symposium LITURGICAL PERSPECTIVES: PRAYER AND POETRY IN LIGHT OF THE DEAD SEA SCROLLS. The Orion Center for the Study of the Dead Sea Scrolls and Associated Literature. Quoted in *Jewish Prayer*, Wikipedia.

37 Systematic Theology. Wikipedia. https://en.wikipedia.org/wiki/Systematic_theology

38 The name Hebrew is used for descendants of Abraham, Isaac and Jacob. Once Jacob's name was changed to "Israel" his descendants were called Children of Israel or Israelites. After the Babylonian Exile they became known as Jews.

39 Ravi Zacharias & Abdu Murray (April 28, 2020). Seeing Jesus from the East. Zondervan Publishers: Grand Rapids, MI.

40 Sean McDowell, Scott Rae (September 24, 2020). Seeing Jesus from the East with Abdu Murray. Think Biblically: Conversation on Faith and Culture. Biola University. https://www.biola.edu/blogs/think-biblically/2020/seeing-jesus-from-the-east

ABOUT THE AUTHOR

Burnette [Bur] Shilling, Ph.D.
Emeritus Faculty, Bowling Green State University
Academic Director, Jerusalem Center for Biblical Studies

 Bur began his career in ministry and academics in 1970 when he served for 14 years as a church youth pastor and a staff evangelist for Youth for Christ.

During this time, Bur founded *Children of the Light*, which became a marquee youth music ministry in the Findlay, Ohio, area. Bur directed the group for 31 of its 41 years, eventually handing the baton to one of the hundreds of alums who had benefited from membership in the group.

While at Youth for Christ, Bur was a contributing writer for the Life Application Bible as part of a team that wrote the life applications of the biblical text found at the bottom of each page. This book is published by Tyndale House and is the best-selling study Bible today.

Later, Bur taught New Testament and Evangelism/Discipleship for 15 years at Findlay's Winebrenner Theological Seminary, where he designed and developed the Doctor of Ministry degree, a professional degree for pastors and church workers. In 1992, he also began to teach in Israel for the Jerusalem Center for Biblical Studies. Bur continues to teach in Israel and other Middle Eastern and European countries, where he explores the impact of geography, history, and culture on the biblical text.

Bur was a Bowling Green (Ohio) State University faculty member for 15 years. In addition to teaching Internet research in an online degree program, he taught a multidisciplinary course exploring the intellectual concepts that contributed to the development of every facet of Western culture.

Bur completed a baccalaureate degree in religion from Taylor University in Indiana, a Master of Divinity degree from Winebrenner Seminary, a Doctor of Ministry degree from Trinity Evangelical Divinity School in Illinois, and a Ph.D. from Bowling Green State University. He also has done post-doctoral study in biblical geography at Trinity.

He and his wife, Cathy, live in Bluffton, Ohio. They have two children and eleven grandchildren. Bur enjoys woodworking and playing golf.

Kaleidoscope Ministries, LLC: http://www.burshilling.com
Facebook Bible Exploration:
   https://www.facebook.com/bibexploration

Made in United States
Cleveland, OH
01 April 2025

15677803R00042